What Do You See?

Written by Louise A. Gikow

Illustrated by George Ulrich

My First
READER

children's press®

A Division of Scholastic Inc.
New York Toronto London Auckland Sydney
Mexico City New Delhi Hong Kong
Danbury, Connecticut

Library of Congress Cataloging-in-Publication Data

Gikow, Louise.
  What do you see? / written by Louise A. Gikow ; illustrated by George Ulrich.
      p. cm. — (My first reader)
  Summary: The children in this book, as well as the reader, are surprised to find that what they think they see is not what is really there.
  ISBN 0-516-25177-5 (lib. bdg.)   0-516-25278-X (pbk.)
  [1. Picture puzzles.] I. Ulrich, George, ill. II. Title. III. Series.
  PZ7.G369Wh 2005
  [E]—dc22
                                      2004010125

1 2 3 4 5 6 7 8 9 10 R 14 13 12 11 10 09 08 07 06 05

Note to Parents and Teachers

Once a reader can recognize and identify the 49 words used to tell this story, he or she will be able to successfully read the entire book. These 49 words are repeated throughout the story, so that young readers will be able to recognize the words easily and understand their meaning.

The 49 words used in this book are:

a	chair	it	standing
am	cloud	look	tall
an	dog	man	that
arm	down	monster	the
at	farm	no	there
bear	floating	now	under
bed	frown	on	up
big	he	owl	upside
bird	head	scarecrow	was
bunny	his	short	with
butterfly	I	sky	
by	in	small	
cat	is	smile	

There is a cat under that big chair!

No, look at it now.

That was a dog under there.

There is a man. The man is tall!

10

No, he is short.
That man is small!

There is an owl. It is up in the sky.

No, look at it now. That is a butterfly.

There is a man with a bird on his arm.

No, that is a scarecrow.
He is on a farm.

19

There is a bunny floating in the sky.

No, that is a cloud that is floating by.

There is a monster under the bed.

No, that is a bear. He is on his head!

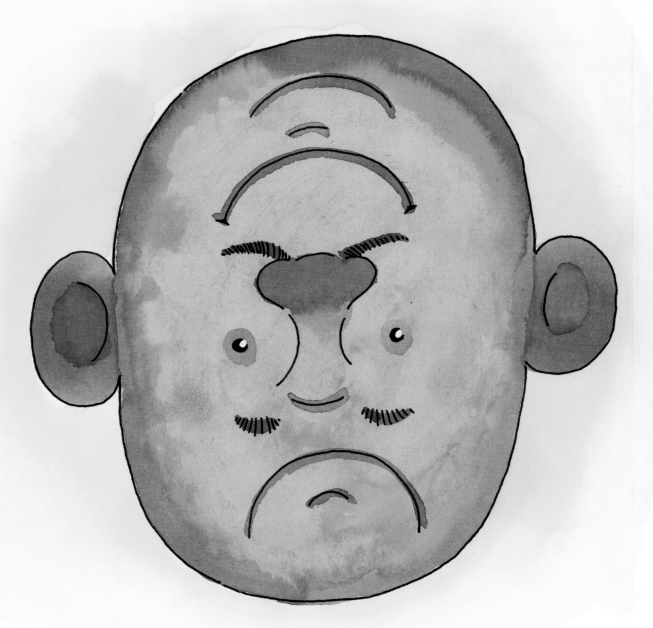

There is a man with a big, big frown.

No, that is a smile!

I am upside down!

ABOUT THE AUTHOR

Louise A. Gikow has written hundreds of books for children (and a few for young adults and grown-ups, too). She has also written songs and scripts for videos and television shows. Most recently, she was a writer for *Between the Lions,* the PBS-Kids TV series that helps children learn to read. This story was hard to write, since she had to think a lot about how the pictures could trick you. She hopes they do (a little!).

ABOUT THE ILLUSTRATOR

George Ulrich was born in Morristown, New Jersey. He graduated from Syracuse University with a degree in Illustration. Since 1973, he has illustrated many children's books, including three that he wrote. George lives in Marblehead, Massachusetts, with his wife, Suzanne, who is also an artist. They have two grown sons and two beautiful grandchildren.